24 Day Countdown Until Christmas Advent Notebook

CREATED BY:

JODIE DILLON

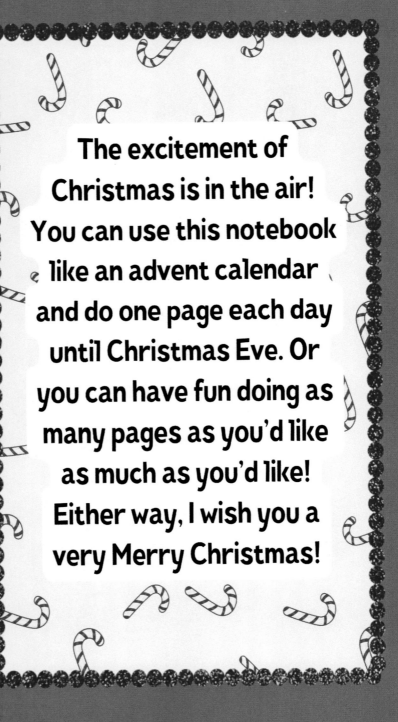

The excitement of Christmas is in the air! You can use this notebook like an advent calendar and do one page each day until Christmas Eve. Or you can have fun doing as many pages as you'd like as much as you'd like! Either way, I wish you a very Merry Christmas!

REASONS WHY I LOVE CHRISTMAS

Write your list below!

COLOR THE CHRISTMAS TREE

CHRISTMAS
TONGUE TWISTERS
CODE BREAKER

A	B	C	D	E	F	G	H	I	J	K	L	M
🧍	🎅	🎩	❄️	🔔	🧢	🔮	🛷	🍬	🎄	🔴	🧦	🎁

N	O	P	Q	R	S	T	U	V	W	X	Y	Z
🕯️	🧥	🧤	👼	⭐	👜	🎀	🍃	🦌	🎄	🔥	⛄	🎍

Can you decode these Christmas tongue twisters? Use the key to break the code

1

(BOBBY BRINGS BIG / BRIGHT BELLS)

2

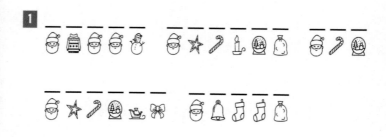

(SEVEN SANTAS / SANG SILLY SONGS)

3

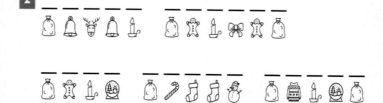

(SILLY SNOWMAN / SLIDES AND SLIPS)

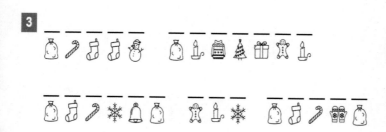

Pass along Christmas joy!
On separate paper, create
3 holiday cards to give to
family and friends.

✳ MERRY ✳

CHRISTMAS

Christmas Word Search

Can you find the words hidden in the puzzle?

```
C  A  N  D  Y  C  A  N  E  R  D  C
H  X  L  P  N  H  F  H  O  S  T  S
J  P  I  C  A  R  O  L  S  I  R  T
I  O  U  N  T  I  L  O  T  C  I  O
N  M  Y  M  G  S  A  N  T  A  C  C
G  S  J  U  M  T  O  H  K  I  K  K
L  T  B  G  S  M  E  R  R  Y  O  I
E  L  F  B  O  A  N  D  K  R  T  N
R  R  P  R  E  S  E  N  T  S  E  G
P  T  R  A  E  I  C  T  T  R  I  S
D  F  C  O  N  F  H  S  A  A  E  N
R  E  I  N  D  E  E  R  X  Y  E  E
```

CANDY CANE	JINGLE	CAROLS	JOY
CHRISTMAS	SANTA	REINDEER	ELF
STOCKINGS	MERRY	PRESENTS	TREE

Dec. 6

Come up with a new elf to help Santa! Fill out his information and color him too!

My elf's name is

His favorite toy to make is

His favorite holiday treat is

Decorate the gingerbread house below!

CHRISTMAS WREATH

Color the Christmas wreath and decorate it using your imagination!

Christmas Symmetry

Draw the other half of this snowflake.

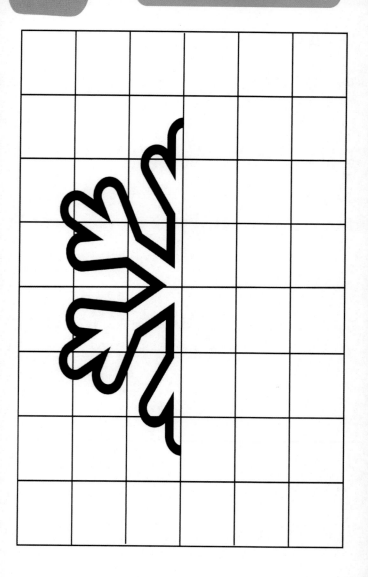

Dec. 10

Dear Santa,

Hello! Hope you are doing great!

My name is _____

I am _____ years old.

I live in _____

I have been very good this year. I

_____

_____

This year for Christmas I would like

1. _____

2. _____

3. _____

I can't wait for you to visit me this year!

Love from,

_____

YUM!

Create a new kind of candy cane.
Show your design below.

Christmas Activities

Play tic tac toe with a friend:

Help the reindeer find the candy cane:

Draw a present you'd like to receive:

LET IT SNOW!

Draw a Christmas scene inside the snow globe.

Christmas

BUCKET LIST

- [ ] BAKE CHRISTMAS COOKIES
- [ ] WATCH CHRISTMAS MOVIE
- [ ] RANDOM ACT OF KINDNESS
- [ ] SEND CHRISTMAS CARD
- [ ] WRITE LETTER TO SANTA
- [ ] MAKE GINGERBREAD HOUSE
- [ ] EAT A CANDY CANE
- [ ] DONATE TO A FOOD DRIVE
- [ ] WEAR CHRISTMAS SOCKS
- [ ] DRINK HOT CHOCOLATE

- [ ] GO ICE SKATING
- [ ] BUILD A SNOWMAN
- [ ] SING CHRISTMAS SONGS
- [ ] PUT ON A COZY SWEATER
- [ ] READ CHRISTMAS BOOK
- [ ] MAKE A PAPER SNOWFLAKE
- [ ] WRAP A PRESENT
- [ ] LEAVE A TREAT FOR ELF ON THE SHELF
- [ ] VISIT FRIENDS OR FAMILY
- [ ] GO SLEDDING

Dec.

16

design a star ornament!

Dec. 18

Stuck In A Snow-globe

Color in the picture and create a story about the snowman above.

_____

_____

_____

_____

_____

_____

_____

_____

_____

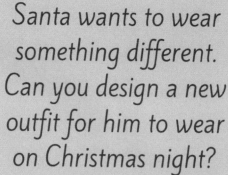

Santa wants to wear something different. Can you design a new outfit for him to wear on Christmas night?

Dec.
20

Santa's reindeer are tired. So the llamas are helping out this year. Color them for the big night!

ROLL A
SNOWMAN

Roll the dice and decorate the snowman

 Draw the eyes

 Draw the nose

 Draw the mouth

 Draw the buttons

 Draw the hat and scarf

 Decorate the arms

STOCKING FILLERS

MAKE A LIST OF ALL THE THINGS YOU'D LIKE IN YOUR STOCKING!

_____

_____

_____

_____

_____

_____

_____

_____

_____

_____

_____

Christmas Poem

Write an acrostic poem about Christmas.

C_____

H_____

R_____

I_____

S_____

T_____

M_____

A_____

S_____

Decorate and color the cookies to leave for Santa tonight!

Christmas Day

SCAVENGER HUNT

- [ ] ORNAMENT
- [ ] MISTLETOE
- [ ] COOKIE
- [ ] ANGEL
- [ ] CANDY CANE
- [ ] WREATH
- [ ] SNOWMAN
- [ ] MITTENS
- [ ] SNOW GLOBE
- [ ] RED BOW
- [ ] SCARF

- [ ] PINE TREE
- [ ] REINDEER
- [ ] SWEATER
- [ ] GOLD OR SILVER BELL
- [ ] SANTA
- [ ] ADVENT CALENDAR
- [ ] STOCKING
- [ ] STAR
- [ ] ELF ON SHELF
- [ ] PRESENTS
- [ ] SNOWFLAKE

USE THESE LAST PAGES TO DRAW AND WRITE WHATEVER YOU LIKE!

notes

Cursive Handwriting

Trace the letters to practice cursive:

a b c d e f g h i

j k l m n o p q

r s t u v v w x y z

Holiday Drawings

Notes:

_____

_____

_____

_____

DATE:

_____

_____

_____

_____

_____

_____

_____

_____

_____

_____

_____

I'd love to hear from you!

Send an email to:
grayfeatherpublishing@gmail.com

Made in the USA
Coppell, TX
02 December 2023

25158450R00026